Chineasy®

WORKBOOK

Chineasy®

WORKBOOK

BY SHAOLAN 曉嵐

with illustrations by NOMA BAR

Thames & Hudson

CONTENTS

INTRODUCTION

Chineasy methodology

The Chinese language is traditionally taught through a series of between roughly 180 and 215 radicals. These radicals are then used to form the characters of the Chinese language. Chineasy has broken down this collection of characters into their most basic and recurring forms, allowing students to learn fewer and simpler radicals that we have termed 'building blocks'.

One building block (e.g. the character 火 for 'fire', see p. 30), or a specific compound form of the building block (e.g. 灬 'fire', see p. 30), can be combined with one or more other characters to make a compound character (e.g. 炎 'burning hot', see p. 31). Two or more independent characters can be placed next to one another to make phrases (e.g. 炎炎 'blazing', see p. 31). In compounds, a whole new character is created; in phrases, the placement of characters next to one another gives a new meaning to the collection of characters. This principle of building blocks is what makes Chineasy so easy!

fire
(building
block)

burning
hot
(compound)

burning hot burning hot

blazing (phrase)

The development of writing styles

Chinese characters have evolved throughout history owing to changes of political regime, geographic expansion and the need to address social progress. There are five major historical Chinese writing styles: 'oracle-bone script' 甲骨文 (c. 1400 BCE), 'bronze script' 金文 (c. 1600–700 BCE), 'seal script' 篆書 (c. 220 BCE), 'clerical script' 隸書 (c. 200 BCE) and 'regular script' 楷書 (often called 'standard script'; c. 200 BCE). You will see references to most of these styles in this book. Each writing style has its own distinct features. Oracle-bone script is a set of characters etched on to animal bones or pieces of turtle shell that were then used for divination. Despite its pictorial nature, it developed into a fully functional and mature writing system. Bronze script (金 means 'gold' or 'metal') refers literally to 'text on metals', as these inscriptions were largely found on ritual bronzes

'sun'/'day' in
oracle bone

'sun'/'day' in
seal script

'sun'/'day' in
clerical script

'sun'/'day' in
regular script

'sun'/'day' in
modern Chinese

such as bells and cauldrons. The development of seal script witnessed the removal of curved or lengthy strokes; Chinese characters written in this style became roughly square in shape. By the time of the introduction of regular script, strokes had become smoother and straighter, and thus the characters were clearer and much easier to read and write.

In modern Chinese, regular script is most commonly used in writing and printing, while the earlier writing styles are used as calligraphic art forms. My calligrapher mother can write poems in seal script, clerical script, regular script and even cursive script (草書). Following the invention of the movable-type process, Song and Ming type styles came into use, just as Arial, Times New Roman and Helvetica are popular typefaces today for alphabetical languages. Nowadays our computers offer dozens of typeface choices.

Spacing

What is the difference between writing a character and a phrase? A character, whether it's a building block or a compound, fits within one square. When you see two people squeezed together in a single square, you know it's a character – for example, the simplified character 'to follow' 从 (see p. 14).

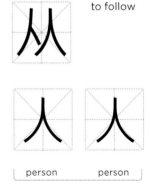

to follow

person　　　person

everyone

A phrase, on the other hand, is spaced across two or more squares. That means, if you see two or more characters spread across two or more squares, then you know it's a phrase – for example, 'everyone' 人人 (see p. 18).

The beauty of the Chineasy method is that you can construct many new 'words' by combining existing characters. Chinese characters rarely appear alone; it is often only in the context of a phrase that the meaning of a character becomes clear. Learning phrases is a giant but easy step towards improving your Chinese study.

Stroke order

Chinese characters usually comprise two or more strokes. When you are writing, it's important to draw these strokes in the correct order.

A particular method of writing characters was developed in CE 300, and since that time every Chinese child has learned how to write using the so-called Eight Principles of Yong (永字八法). There are eight common strokes you see in written Chinese. The character 永 (yong^3), which means 'forever', is often used to demonstrate these strokes.

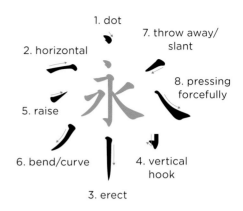

1. 點/点 (dian^3; dot)
2. 橫 (heng^2; horizontal) Draw this stroke from left to right. If a character has more than two horizontal strokes, always draw the top one first.
3. 豎 (shu^4; erect) A vertical line drawn from top to bottom.
4. 豎鈎 (shu^4 gou^1; vertical hook) This stroke looks the same as 豎 except for the tiny hook at the bottom.
5. 提 (ti^2; raise) A flick up and to the right.
6. 彎/弯 (wan^1; bend/curve) A tapering curve, usually down to the left, and drawn quickly.
7. 撇 (pie^3; throw away/slant) A short, downwards stroke, always drawn from right to left.
8. 捺 (na^4; pressing forcefully) Start at the top and move to the bottom right. You can lift your pen a bit towards the end.

Speaking

To teach Mandarin Chinese to non-native speakers, most teachers use pinyin, the standard phonetic system for transcribing the sound of Chinese characters in the romanized alphabet. Chinese is a tonal language, so the pinyin system uses a series of either numerals or glyphs to represent tone. For instance, the pinyin for 'person' can be written as either ren^2 or rén. Chineasy uses the numerical pinyin system. After every English translation, you will see a word in brackets followed by a number; this acts as a guide to the pronunciation of the character. See, for example, p. 13 人 person (ren^2).

Tone 1 = high level tone
Tone 2 = medium rising tone
Tone 3 = falling rising tone
Tone 4 = falling tone
No number = neutral tone

Direction

Is Chinese written horizontally or vertically? Chinese can be written in either direction. You can read from left to right, right to left, or top to bottom. The only direction you won't find is bottom to top. Today the most common style is from left to right, in the same way that English, French, Spanish or German are read.

In some ancient literature or on road signs in China, you will sometimes see phrases written from right to left. This can prove to be odd when you have literature that mixes both English and Chinese. I once saw a book cover that had the English title running from left to right and the Chinese title running from right to left!

If you are trying to read vertically (for example, you quite often have to do this if you are reading scrolls), then you would read from right to left, starting with the first vertical line on the right from top to bottom, and then moving towards the left of the scroll.

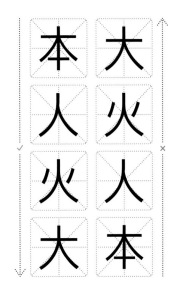

本人火大 I am furious
(ben³ ren² huo³ da⁴)

one's self + angry =
[literally] one is angry = I am furious

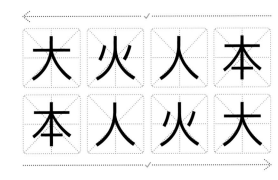

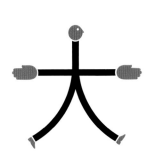

foundation/origin   person   fire   big

I am furious

WORKBOOK

人 person

口 mouth

水 water

火 fire

木 tree

山 mountain

日 sun/day

月 moon/month

夕 dusk

女 woman

男 man

父 father

母 mother

子 son/child

生 birth/life

戶 household

田 field

門 door

馬 horse

羊 sheep

牛 cow

犬 dog

龙 dragon

虎 tiger

鳥 bird

手 hand

足 foot

左 left 右 right

目 eye

耳 ear

头 head

发 hair

人 person (ren²)

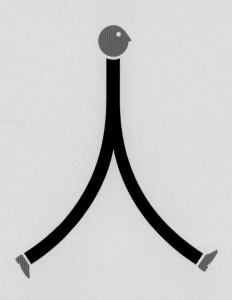

从 to follow (cong²)

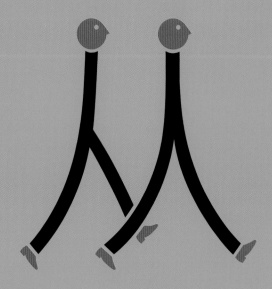

Practise drawing the character for person in the grid below.
Remember to draw the strokes in the correct order, as shown.

人 person (ren²)

Hello, people! Our first building block is 'person'. This building block traditionally depicted a human in profile. Today it looks like the profile of a man walking. 亻 is the form of the character used as a component in certain compounds.

There are lots of compound characters you can make using the character for person. Practise writing these below, using the grids to help you space the different elements correctly.

从 to follow (cong²)

This character comprises two building blocks for 'person'. One man leads, the other follows close behind. This is the simplified form; the traditional form of this character is 從.

众 crowd (zhong⁴)

'Two's company, three's a crowd.' Three building blocks for 'person' make a crowd. This is the simplified form; the traditional form of this character is 眾.

大 big (da[4])

This character depicts a
man stretching his arms
wide. Imagine that he is
saying, 'It was this big'.

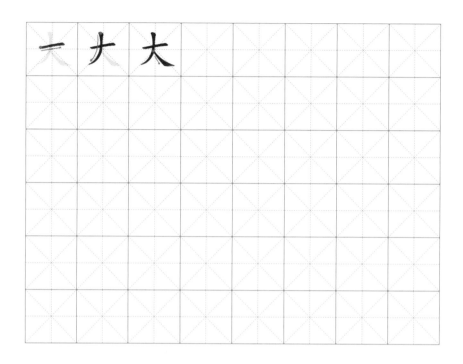

太 too much (tai[4])

This compound comprises
'big' and a stroke under
the character, suggesting
something even bigger.
It also means 'extremely'
or 'excessively'.

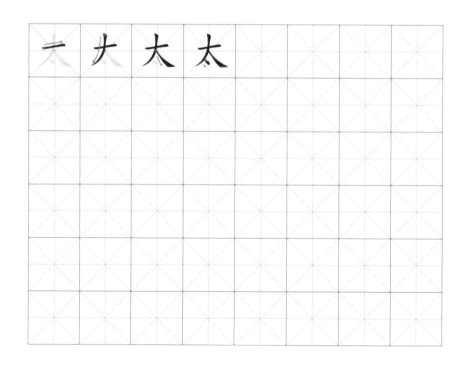

天 sky (tian[1])

In oracle-bone script, this character depicted a person with a head. In seal script, the head developed into a horizontal line, indicating the sky above one's head. So now this character is formed by 'one' (see p. 49) and 'big', showing a man opening his arms (**大**) and standing beneath the sky (**一**). It can also mean 'day' or 'heaven'.

Now try writing out some of the phrases that can be made using the compound characters of 人. Use the grid to help you space the characters evenly.

人人 everyone
(ren² ren²)

person + person = everyone

If we double up 'person', we have 'everyone'.
For stroke order see p. 13.

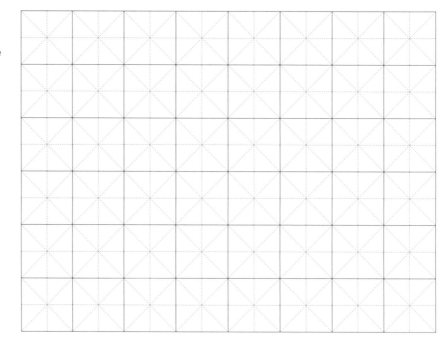

大人 adult
(da⁴ ren²)

big + person = adult

The modern meaning of 'big-size person' is 'adult'. Traditionally, this phrase referred to people who were of higher social or official rank. For stroke order see pp. 16 and 13.

众人 people
(zhong[4] ren[2])

crowd + person = people

A crowd is made up of many different people. This phrase also means 'everybody'.
For stroke order
see pp. 15 and 13.

大众 public
(da[4] zhong[4])

big + crowd = public

A big crowd forms
the public.
For stroke order
see pp. 16 and 15.

大 big (da⁴)

太 too much (tai⁴)

天大 extremely big
(tian[1] da[4])

What could be a bigger
space than the heavens?
sky + big = [literally] big
as the sky = extremely big
For stroke order see
pp. 17 and 16.

太大 too big
(tai[4] da[4])

A straightforward phrase:
if something is too big,
there is too much of it.
too much + big = too big
For stroke order see p. 16.

Our next building block is 'mouth' or 'to surround'. Practise drawing the character in the grid below.

口 mouth (kou³)

Depending on the size of the building block, this character means either 'mouth' (if it is small) or 'to surround' (if it is large).

Here are some compound characters you can make using 口.

回 to return (hui[2])

This character is a combination of a small 'mouth' and 'to surround'. Imagine that it depicts a swirling whirlpool, continuously turning back on itself.

品 quality (pin³)

Imagine that each mouth is an opinion. The quality of something is judged by what people say about it. This character also means 'item', 'product' or 'grade'.

因 to cause (yin[1])

This character is a combination of 'mouth' and 'big'. It also means 'because of' and 'reason'. I like to remember it by thinking that a big mouth causes problems (although, in this case, 口 means 'to surround').

You can also create phrases by combining the characters for 'person' and 'mouth', or their compounds.

人口 population
(ren[2] kou[3])

When we start counting how many mouths we need to feed, we are talking about population.
person + mouth = population
For stroke order see pp. 13 and 22.

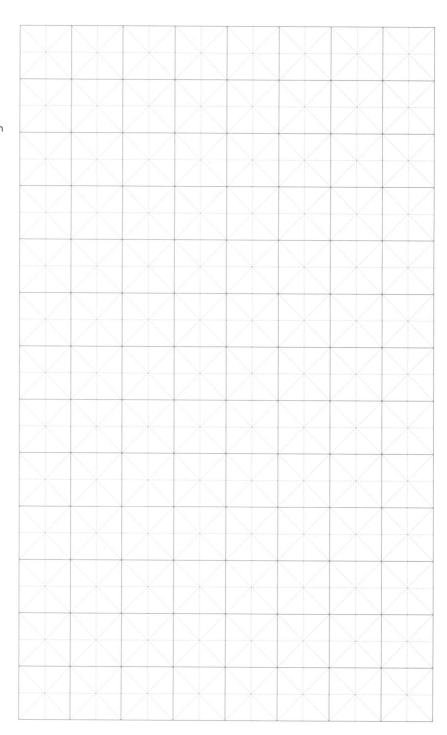

人品 morality
(ren² pin³)

Remember, it is always
wise to judge the quality
of a person on the basis
of their morality.
person + quality = morality
For stroke order see
pp. 13 and 24.

水 water (shui³)

Practise writing the character for 'water' in the grid below.

水 water (shui[3])

The building block for 'water' looks like a winding river, with streams entering into it on either side. 氵 is the form of the character used as a component in certain compounds.

Practise writing the character for 'fire' and its compounds in the grids.

火 fire (huo³)

The building block for 'fire' represents a central flame with a smaller spark on either side. It reminds me of a campfire. I like to remember this character by thinking about a person waving their arms, saying, 'Help! I'm on fire!'

灬 is the form of the character used as a component in certain compounds.

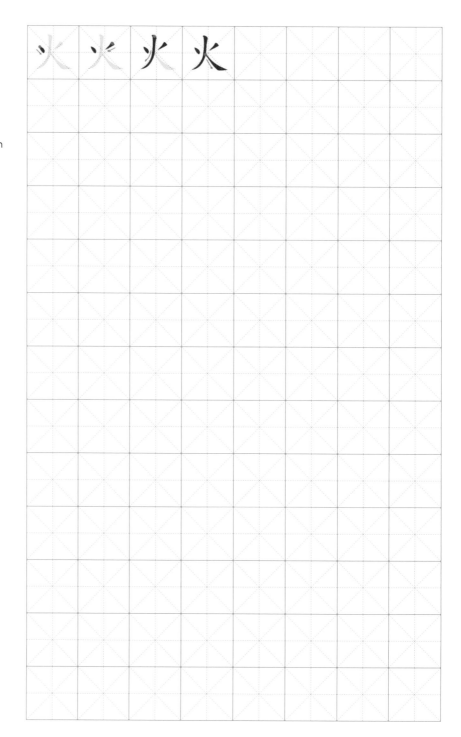

炎 burning hot (yan[2])

This compound comprises two 'fire' building blocks stacked on top of each other. They are burning twice as hot as before. This character also means 'inflammation'.

Placing two of these characters side by side makes the phrase 'blazing'.

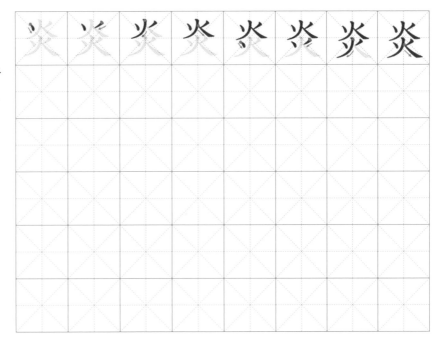

淡 plain (dan[4])

This character is a combination of 'water' and 'burning hot'. It also means 'light', 'bland', 'modest', 'essential' or 'tasteless'.

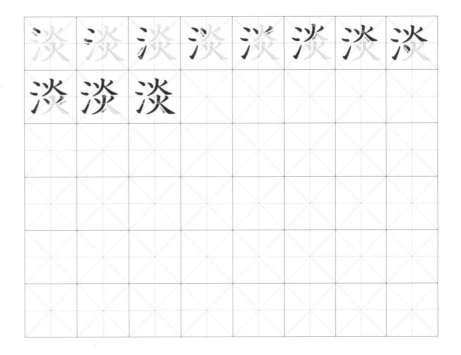

伙 group (huo³)

In ancient China, fires were used mainly for cooking and for warmth. When people gathered around the fire, they were considered to be part of the group.

火大 angry
(hou³ da⁴)

When a person burns
with rage, we can assume
that they are angry. This
is quite an informal term.
fire + big = angry
For stroke order see
pp. 30 and 16.

大火 big fire
(da⁴ hou³)

Switching the order
of the characters changes
the meaning of the phrase.
big + fire = big fire
For stroke order see
pp. 16 and 30.

Practise writing the character for 'tree' and its compounds in the grids below.

木 tree (mu[4])

The building block for 'tree' represents a tree trunk with hanging branches. When this character is used as an adjective, it refers to a wooden texture. When it is used to describe a person, it means 'clumsy', 'dumb' or 'numb'.

本 foundation (ben³)

The foundation of a house is the first step in its construction, and traditionally foundations were made of wood. This character also means 'origin'.

來 to come (lai²)

This character is a combination of 'tree' and two 'person' building blocks. In ancient China, 'to come' was represented by a character based on wheat, which had been brought to China from Europe. The simplified form is 来.

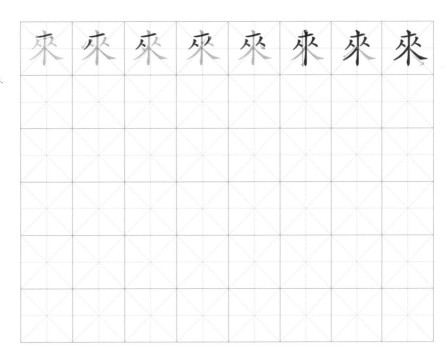

休 rest (xiu[1])

This character is a combination of 'person' and 'tree'. I like to remember it by imagining a person resting against a tree.

体 body (ti³)

This character is a combination of 'person' and 'foundation'. A person's foundation is their body. This is the simplified form; the traditional form is 體.

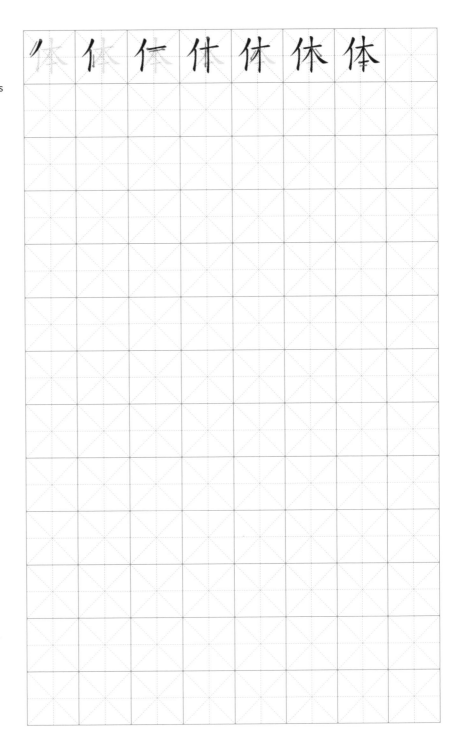

Try writing these phrases, using the grids to help you space the characters correctly.

大体 in general
(da[4] ti[3])

This phrase can be used to mean 'in general', 'more or less' or 'basically'.
big + body = in general
For stroke order see pp. 16 and 37.

本人 one's self
(ben[3] ren[2])

Remember: a person's origin often influences their sense of self.
origin + person = [literally] person's origin = one's self
For stroke order see pp. 35 and 13.

來人 messenger
(lai[2] ren[2])

Before the age of electricity, all messages had to be sent by person. This is quite an old-fashioned or poetical phrase.
to come + person = messenger
For stroke order see pp. 35 and 13.

You can build new phrases by combining the characters 回 and 來 in different orders. Notice how the order changes the meaning.

回來 to come back
(hui² lai²)

to return + to come =
[literally] to return from
where you have come
= to come back.
For stroke order
see pp. 23 and 35.

來回 round trip
(lai² hui²)

to come + to return =
[literally] to return to where
you have come = round trip.
For stroke order see pp. 35
and 23.

Now you can write a full sentence using the characters you've learnt so far.

本人火大 I am furious
(ben³ ren² huo³ da⁴)

one's self + angry =
[literally] one is angry
= I am furious.
For stroke order see
pp. 35, 13, 30 and 16.

Practise writing the character for 'mountain' and its compounds in the grids.

山 mountain (shan[1])

The character for 'mountain' represents the peaks of a mountain range.

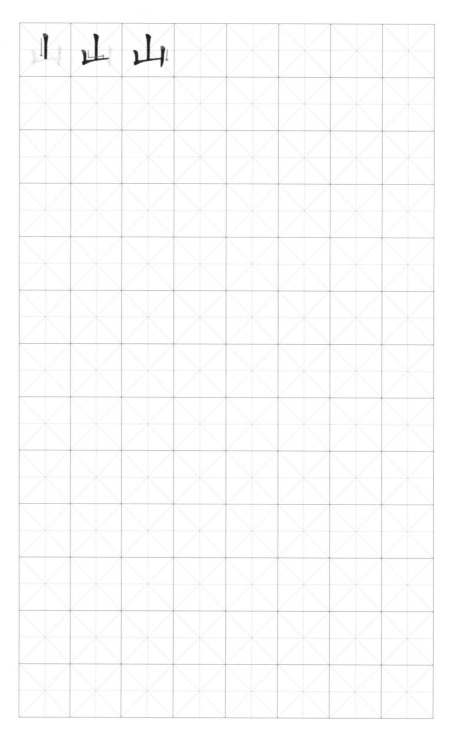

出 to get out (chu¹)

In the past, the Emperor sent people into exile beyond the mountains. As a result, this character used to mean 'exit'. Today it means 'to get out'.

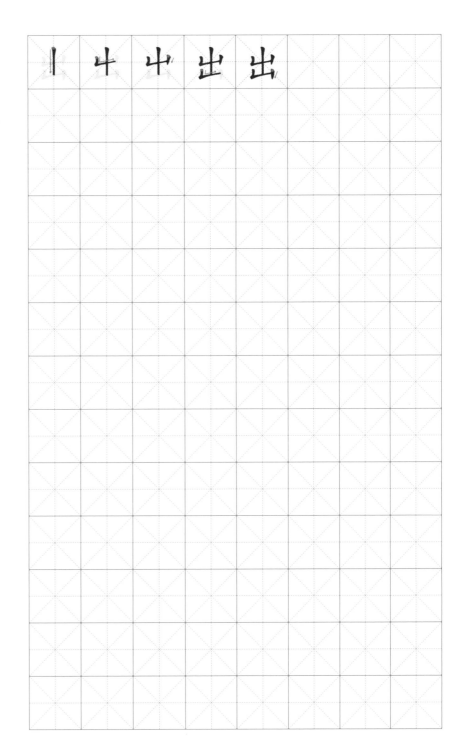

Combining the characters for 'fire' and 'mountain' creates
a new phrase.

火山 volcano
(huo³ shan¹)

fire + mountain = volcano
For stroke order see
pp. 30 and 42.

火山 volcano (huo³ shan¹)

大火 big fire (da⁴ hou³)

女 woman (nü³)

男 man/male (nan²)

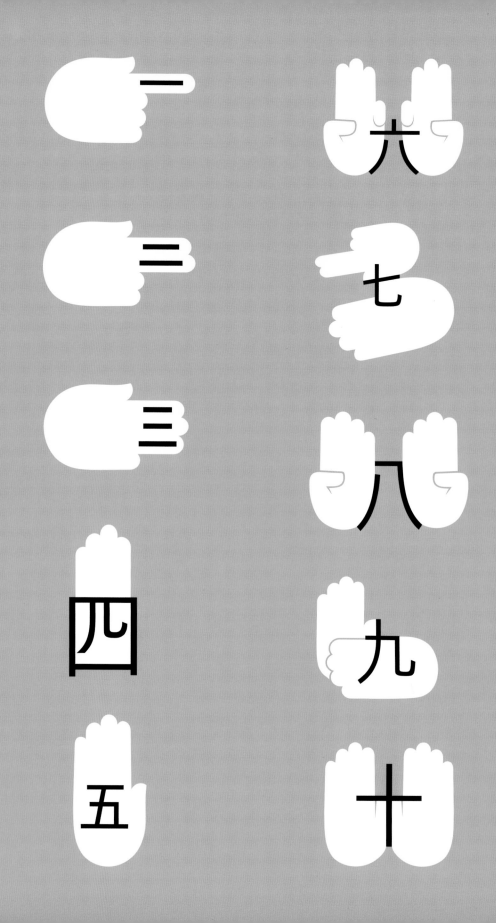

Now practise writing the numbers 1 to 10.

一 one (yi¹)

The character for 'one' is a simple horizontal line.

二 two (er⁴)

The character for 'two' is as easy as the number one!

三 three (san¹)

The character for 'three' continues the simple pattern of 'one' and 'two' by adding a third stroke, thus 三.

四 four (si⁴)

The number four is considered unlucky because it sounds very similar to 'death' 死 (si³).

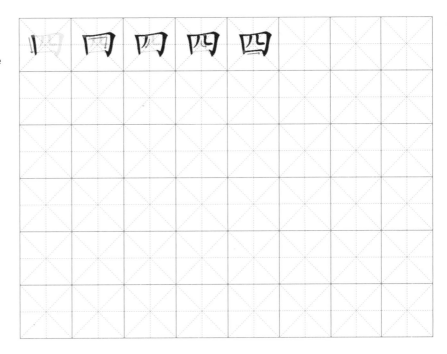

五 five (wu³)

This number is associated with the five elements and the Emperor of China.

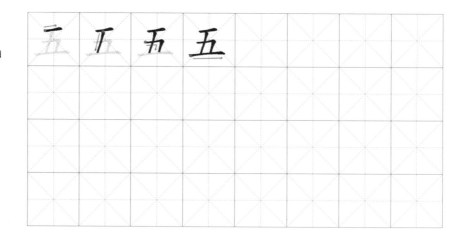

六 six (liu⁴)

Originally, this character was a pictograph of a hut, but now 六 is used exclusively to mean 'six' – a lucky number in China, especially in business.

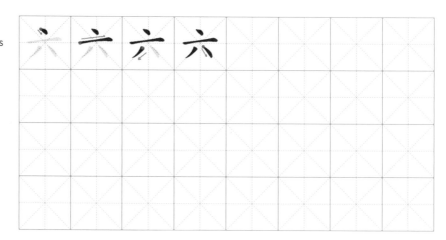

七 seven (qi¹)

Seven symbolizes 'togetherness', and is auspicious for relationships.

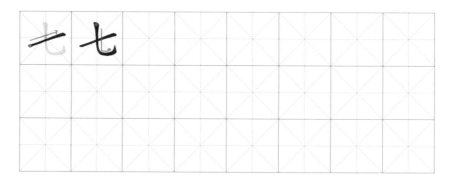

八 eight (ba[1])

In the Mandarin and Cantonese dialects, the number eight sounds very similar to 'prosperity' and 'fortune' respectively, which makes it a very lucky number throughout the Chinese-speaking world.

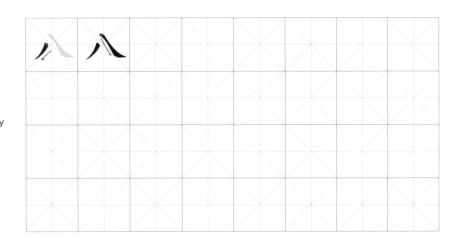

九 nine (jiu[3])

The number nine is also considered auspicious because it's associated with the Emperor (and with dragons!) and sounds the same as 'long-lasting' 久 (jiu[3]).

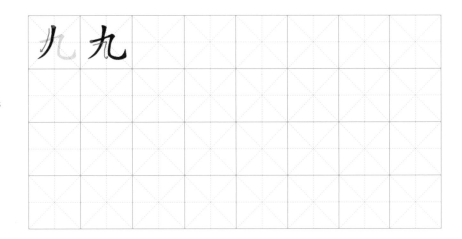

十 ten (shi[2])

In oracle-bone inscriptions, 'ten' was represented by a simple vertical line or sometimes a vertical line with a dot in the middle, which was itself a reference to an ancient way of indicating 'ten' by tying a knot in a rope.

Practise writing the character for 'sun' or 'day' in the grid below.

日 sun/day (ri⁴)

In oracle-bone and seal inscriptions, the character for 'sun' was a circle with a dot in the middle. It has since evolved to look very similar to a Western window. This character also means 'day'.

The compounds of 日 have meanings that are closely related to both 'sun' and 'day'.

旦 sunrise (dan⁴)

This is an easy compound to remember, as it depicts the sun rising above the line of the horizon.

東 east (dong¹)

This character is a combination of 'tree' and 'sun'. The sun rises in the East, and a man would have first glimpsed the sun through the trees. The simplified form is 东.

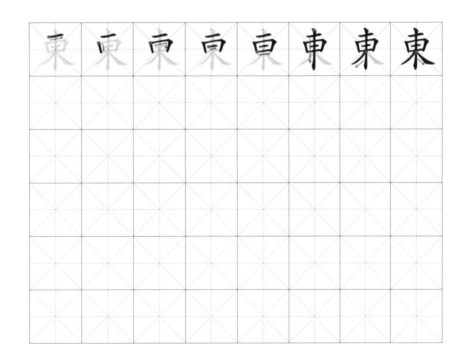

Practise writing the character for 'moon' in the grid below.

月 moon/month (yue[4])

The traditional Chinese calendar is based on the lunar cycle, so in addition to meaning 'moon', the character 月 also means 'month'.

月 moon/month (yue⁴)

The character for 'origin' can be used to qualify 'day' or 'month'.

本日 today (ben³ ri⁴)

origin + day = today
If you swap the order of
the characters, this phrase
means 'Japan'. Japan lies
to the east of China, which
is where the sun rises.
For stroke order see
pp. 35 and 52.

本月 this month
(ben[3] yue[4])

origin + month = this month.
For stroke order see pp. 35
and 54.

Combining the characters for 'sun' and 'moon' creates a new compound.

明 bright (ming[2])

When the sun and moon shine together, it creates a character meaning 'bright' or 'brightness'. This character also means 'tomorrow'.

You can combine characters you've already learnt to refer to days in the future.

明日 tomorrow
(ming[2] ri[4])

Remember, after a day and a night comes tomorrow. bright + day = tomorrow. For stroke order see pp. 58 and 52.

來日 in the coming days (lai² ri⁴)

to come + day =
in the coming days.
For stroke order see
pp. 35 and 52.

Practise writing the character for 'dusk' in the grid below.

夕 dusk (xi[1])

This character represents the setting sun, and also means 'evening' or 'sunset'.

Here are some compound characters you can make using 夕.

多 many (duo[1])

This character comprises two 'dusk' building blocks, suggesting the accumulation of time. Accumulation implies 'many'.

梦 dream (meng[4])

This character is a combination of 'woods' (a compound of two trees) and 'dusk'. It is the simplified form; the traditional form 夢 includes the characters for 'eye' 目 (see p. 113) and 'dusk' 夕, indicating a person with their eyes closed having a dream.

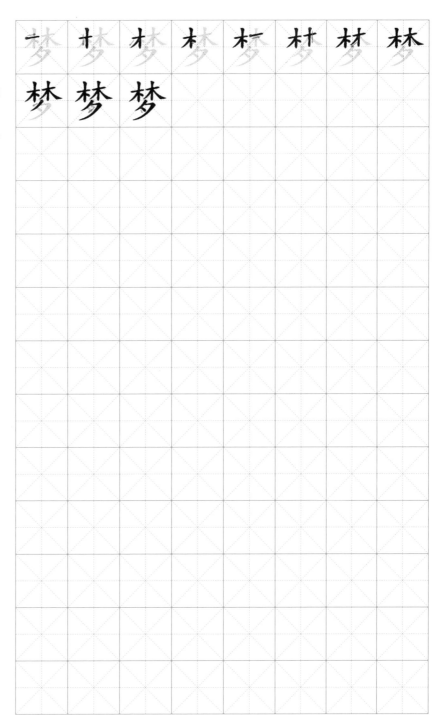

岁 years (sui[4])

This character is a combination of 'mountain' and 'dusk'. It is the simplified form; the traditional form is 歲. The most common usage of 歲 is to count a person's age; for example, 一歲 means 'one year old'.

名 name (ming[2])

This character is a combination of 'dusk' and 'mouth'. It alludes to parents calling their children's names as evening fell. The compound also means 'famous'.

Now practise writing characters about people and families.

女 woman (nü³)

This character traditionally depicted an outline of a woman kneeling on the floor, showing her obedience to a man. I am very frustrated by the origin of this character! When used as an adjective, it means 'female'.
When used in the context of family relationships, this character means 'daughter'.

男 man (nan[2])

In oracle-bone inscriptions, this character depicted a strong man carrying out work in a field. When used as an adjective, this character means 'male'.

父 father (fu[4])

This character depicts a hand holding an axe. In ancient China, the father was the person who used an axe to chop wood for the family, keeping them warm.

母 mother (mu³)

Since its earliest recorded form in oracle-bone inscriptions, this character has depicted a mother's breasts, in reference to feeding a baby. The original forms showed a woman on her knees or standing, but the modern form has shifted vertically and lost the long strokes that represented legs. I bet you'll remember 母 very easily now you know how it got its shape! This character also means 'female' when referring to animals.

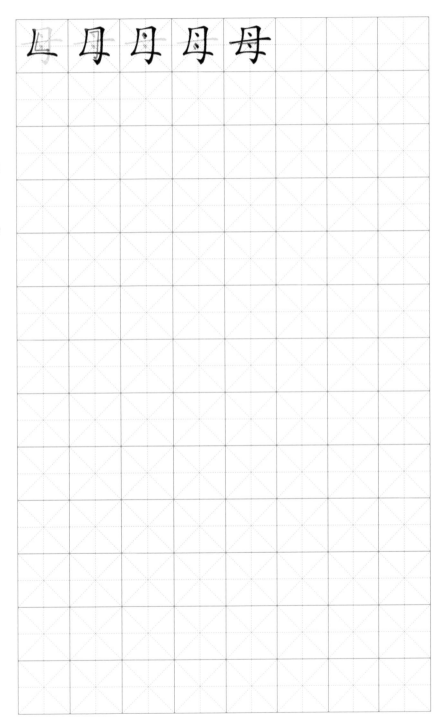

子 son (zi^3)

The earliest form of this character, in oracle-bone inscriptions, depicted a baby with a head, two arms and one leg, and meant 'baby' or 'infant'. The character has now been extended to mean 'son' or 'child'.

生 birth/life (sheng[1])

The original form of this character depicted a handful of sprouts emerging from the earth. The idea of shooting sprouts was extended to the current meaning: 'birth', 'life', 'to be born', 'to give birth', 'to grow' or 'to generate'.

Here are some of the compounds you can make using 女. You can see how they relate to traditional Chinese ideas about women.

好 good (hao³)

This character is a combination of 'woman' and 'son'. In ancient China, the foremost requirement of a good woman was to bear a son in order to continue her husband's line. The character can also mean 'such'.

如 to obey (ru[2])

This character is a combination of 'woman' and 'mouth'. In ancient China, a woman didn't speak her own opinions, she obeyed. This compound also means 'is like'.

Practise writing the characters for 'household' and 'field'.

戶 household (hu⁴)

This character represents a door with one panel. It can be used to refer to either a door or a window, but is most commonly used to mean 'household'. Its simplified form is 户.

田 field (tian[2])

This character depicts a piece of farmland on which criss-cross ditches have been dug for irrigation. It means 'field' or 'farm', and is also a building block for characters relating to farming and hunting.

Practise writing the character for 'door' and its compounds in the grids.

門 door (men²)

The building block for 'door' looks very similar to a pair of saloon doors from the Wild West. Saloon doors may be a much more recent invention, but the resemblance is uncanny! The simplified form is 门.

閃 to dodge (shan[3])

Imagine a person running through a pair of saloon doors, trying to dodge arrest. This character also means 'flash'. The simplified form is 闪.

問 to ask (wen⁴)

This character is a combination of 'door' and 'mouth'. To ask a question is the door to knowledge. The simplified form is 问.

間 space/room (jian[1])

This character is a combination of 'door' and 'sun'. In seal script this character was identical to 閒 'leisure', so it was changed to prevent confusion. The simplified form is 间.

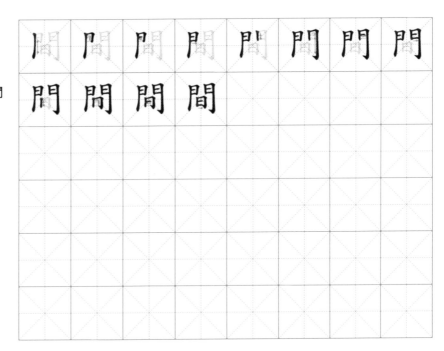

閒 leisure (xian[2])

Before electricity, all work stopped when darkness fell and the moon rose. This character also means 'idle', 'peaceful' or 'calm'. Alternative forms are 閑 and 闲.

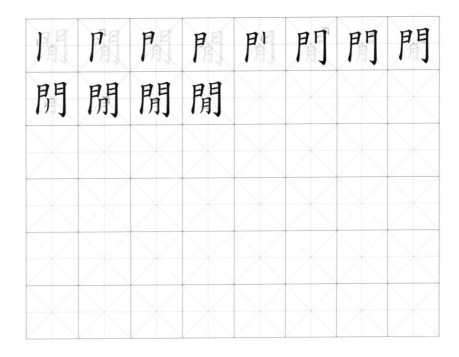

Here are some phrases you can create using compounds of 'door'.

人間 world (ren² jian¹)

person + space = [literally]
the space for people = world
For stroke order see
pp. 13 and 79.

閃人 to sneak out
(shan³ ren²)

to dodge + person =
[literally] person dodging
= to sneak out
For stroke order see
pp. 77 and 13.

間 space/room (jian[1])

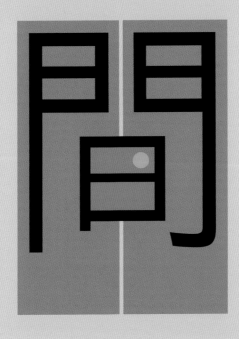

閒 leisure (xian[2])

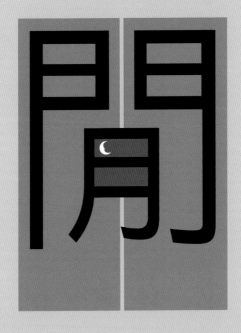

犬 dog (quan³)
鳥 bird (niao³)
羊 sheep (yang²)

牛 cow (niu²)

馬 horse (ma³)

Now practise writing the characters for different animals and their compounds.

馬 horse (ma³)

This building block traditionally looked like a horse on its side. Today you can see only the horse's torso, tail and legs. The simplified form is 马.

羊 sheep (yang²)

In Chinese, 羊 represents the goat-antelope group of mammals. The context, within a phrase or compound, determines if it refers to a sheep, goat or other animal. If you see 'sheep' in a compound character, it tends to relate to something sheep-like or nice and positive.

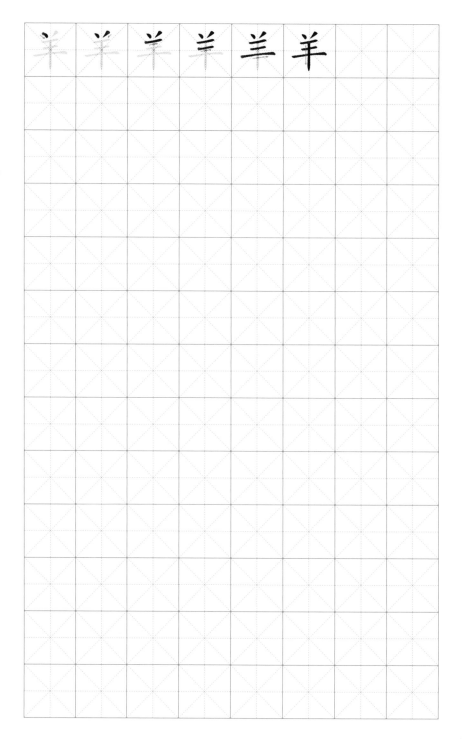

美 beautiful (mei[3])

This character is a combination of 'sheep' and 'big'. In ancient China, sheep were considered auspicious.

牛 cow (niu²)

The original meaning of this character was 'ox', but since the clerical change in writing styles it has meant 'cow'. If you see 'cow' in a character, it tends to relate to stubbornness.

牜 is the form of the character used as a component in certain compounds.

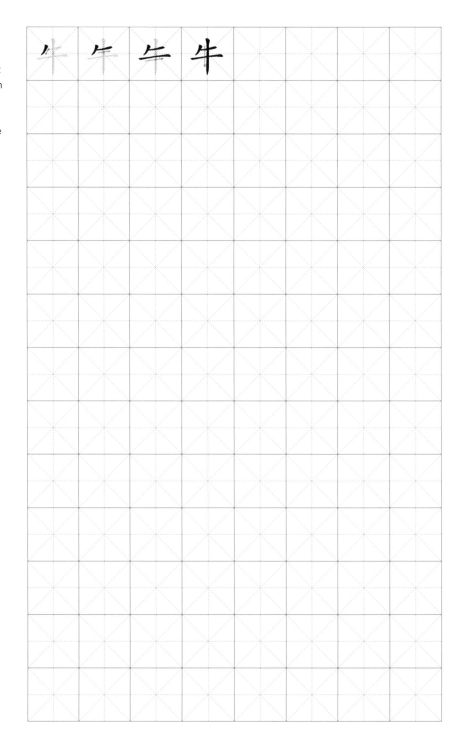

水牛 buffalo
(shui³ niu²)

water + cow = [literally]
water cow = buffalo
The water buffalo with
a large crescent horn is
a major domestic animal
used in southern China
for paddy cultivation.
For stroke order see
pp. 29 and 88.

犬 dog (quan³)

The regular form of this character is 'big' 大 with an additional dot on the upper right side. The earliest form in oracle-bone inscriptions was a drawing of a dog, with the extra stroke representing its tail. 犭 is the form of the character used as a component in certain compounds.

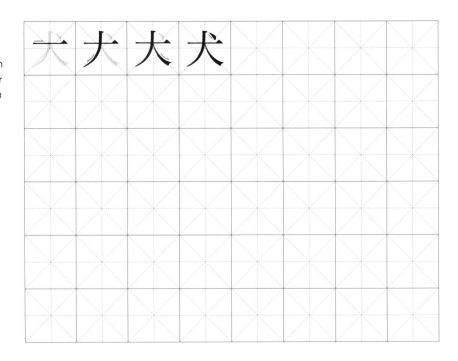

狗 dog (gou³)

The more commonly used character for 'dog' is a combination of 犭, indicating the meaning, and 'sentence' 句 (ju⁴), indicating the pronunciation.

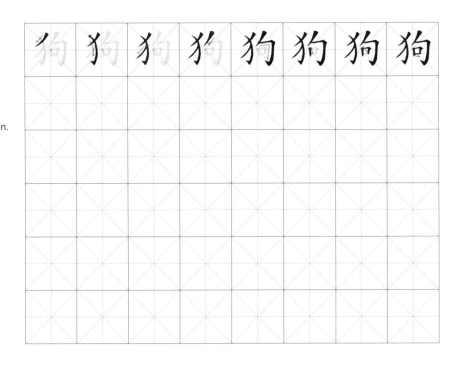

Here are some compounds you can create using 犬.

器 utensil (qi[4])

This character is a combination of 'dog' and four 'mouth' building blocks. It can also mean 'instrument'.

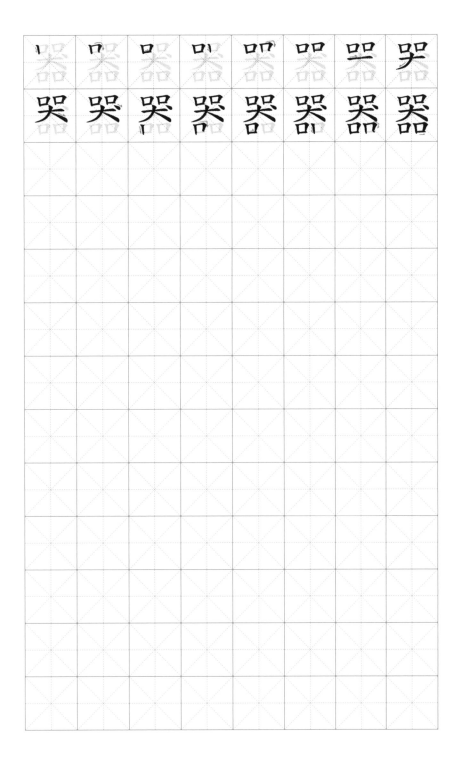

吠 to bark (fei[4])

This character is a combination of 'mouth' and 'dog'. When a dog opens its mouth to emit a sound, it is barking.

哭 to cry (ku[1])

This character is a combination of 'dog' and two 'mouth' building blocks. As the crying sound of a human sounds similar to the whine of a dog, this character means 'to cry'.

You can add the character for 'big' to show that the sound being made is louder.

大吠 to bark loudly
(da[4] fei[4])

big + to bark = [literally]
big bark = to bark loudly
For stroke order see
pp. 16 and 92.

大哭 to cry out
(da⁴ ku¹)

This phrase can also
mean 'to burst into tears'.
big + to cry = [literally]
big cry = to cry out
For stroke order see
pp. 16 and 93.

龙 dragon (long²)

龙 dragon (long[2])

The dragon is probably the most important and symbolic animal in Chinese history. Chinese people call themselves 'the descendants of the dragon'. This legendary creature has the antlers of a deer, the head of a crocodile, the eyes of a demon, the neck of a snake, the viscera of a tortoise, the claws of a hawk, the palms of a tiger and the ears of a cow.

龙 is the simplified form of 'dragon'; the traditional form is 龍.

虎 tiger (hu³)

虎 is one of the pictographic characters from ancient China. When it is used as an adjective, it means 'brave'.

唬 to scare (hu³)

This character is a combination of 'mouth' and 'tiger'. Imagine how scared you would be to hear a tiger roar in the middle of the night.

鳥 bird (niao³)

In oracle-bone and seal inscriptions, this character depicted a bird. The modern character represents a bird with four talons and a hanging tail feather. The simplified form of this character is 鸟.

鳥 bird (niao³)

发 hair (fa³)

头 head (tou²)

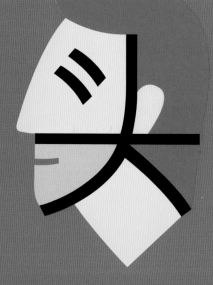

足 foot (zu²)

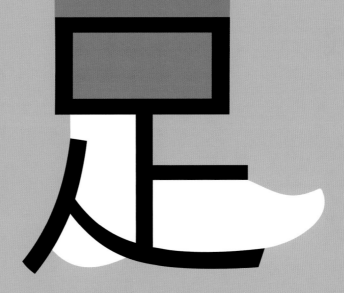

人体 human body (ren² ti³)

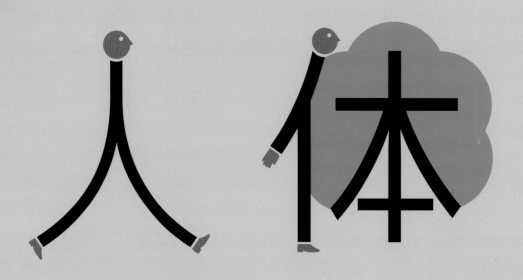

手 hand (shou³)

Practise writing the characters for different parts of the body.

人体 human body
(ren[2] ti[3])

person + body =
human body.
For stroke order
see pp. 13 and 37.

手 hand (shou³)

In oracle-bone inscriptions, the form of this character was an abstract depiction of five fingers with the lower part of the arm. 扌 is the form of the character used as a component in certain compounds.

足 foot (zu²)

The character for 'foot' originally also meant 'to levy troops'. This is logical, since the major force in an army was the infantry – the foot soldiers. (Later, another character was created to mean specifically 'to levy troops'.) The ancient symbol for 足 represented the entire leg; it is only in modern times that the character has come to mean 'foot'.

Here are some of the phrases and compounds you can make using 手.

手足 siblings
(shou³ zu²)

The closest people to us, genetically speaking, are probably our siblings – unless you have a clone! To express the intimacy between siblings, the phrase 'hand and foot' is used to refer to brothers and sisters. It's a very commonly used phrase and an elegant expression to know. For stroke order see pp. 106 and 107.

扶 to assist (fu[2])

This character's composition symbolizes a man being supported by a helping hand. It can also mean 'to support', 'to help', 'to protect' and 'to hold on'.

Now practise writing the characters for 'left' and 'right'. You can combine these with the characters for different body parts. For example, 右手 means 'right hand'.

左 left (zuo³)

In oracle-bone inscriptions, this character depicted a left hand. Later, its meaning became simply 'left'; however, the trace of 'left hand' can still be seen in the modern form of the character, in the component ナ.

右 right (you⁴)

The character for 'right'
has an ancient origin similar
to that of the character
for 'left', 左; originally, the
character 右 depicted a
right hand. The component
'mouth' 口 was added later
at the bottom, and because
of 口, I remember this
character by thinking that,
as a right-handed person,
I use my 'right' 右 hand
when I'm eating.

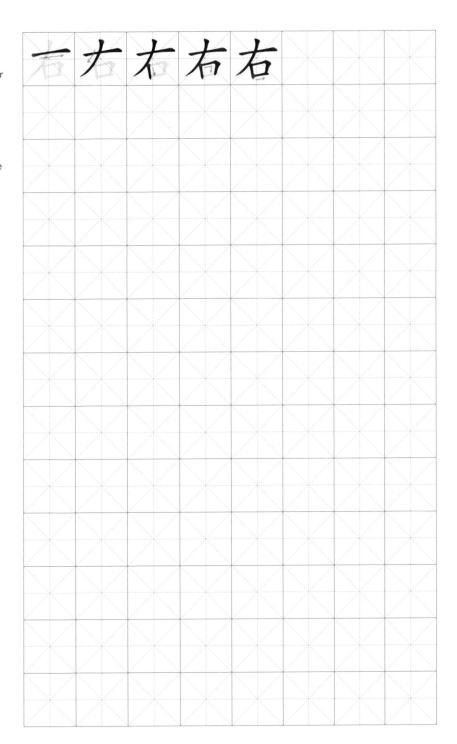

目 eye (mu⁴)

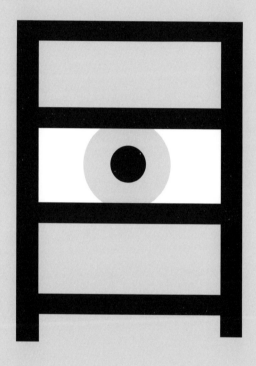

目 eye (mu⁴)

Originally, this character was a pictograph of a human eye and, in comparison to its modern form, it was rotated 90 degrees in a clockwise direction and had curvier lines. As the Chinese language evolved, many characters that were primarily circular or had many curved lines were straightened out in order to make them easier to write.

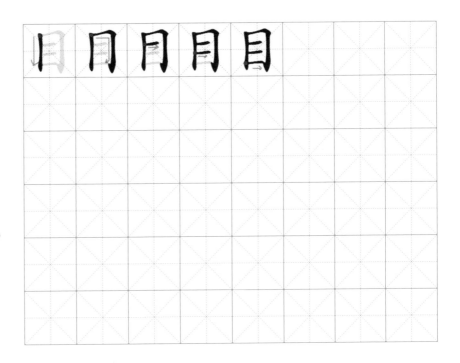

自 oneself (zi⁴)

If you add a dot on top of 'eye', it means 'self' or 'oneself'. This additional stroke should be drawn first, then follow the stroke order for 'eye' above.

耳 ear (er[3])

耳 is one of the ancient Chinese pictographs; the original form looked just like an ear. You can imagine that the opening of the ear is the outer box (口), the cartilage inside the ear is the horizontal lines (二) inside the box, and the earlobe is on the lower right (十).

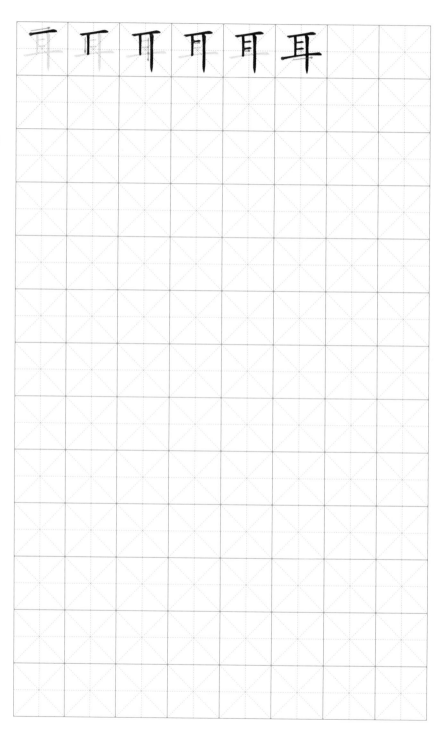

耳目 spy (er[3] mu[4])

An 'ear' and an 'eye'
together make the phrase
for 'intelligence' or 'spy'.
When you have eyes and
ears everywhere, you
collect intelligence.
For stroke order see
pp. 113 and 114.

头 head (tou[2])

Many simplified characters were not introduced until 1949, when the Communist Party took control of mainland China. However, the character for 'head' is a different story. The modern simplified version, **头**, which looks like two dots on top of 'big' **大**, has been in use for thousands of years.

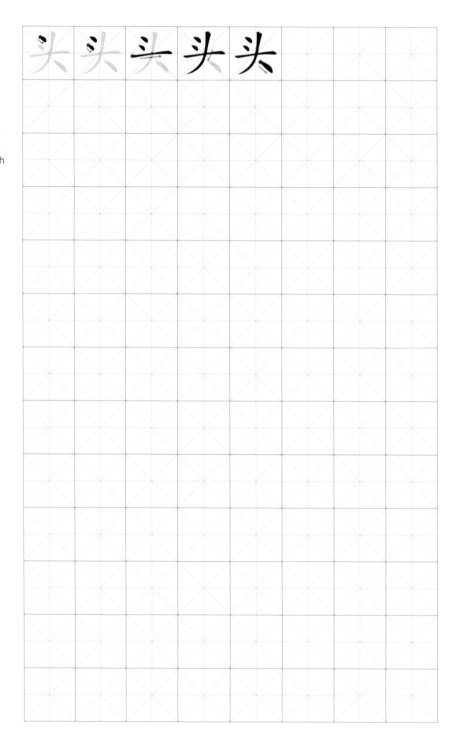

发 hair (fa[3])

发 is the simplified form of two very useful characters: 'hair' 髮 and 'to start' 發.

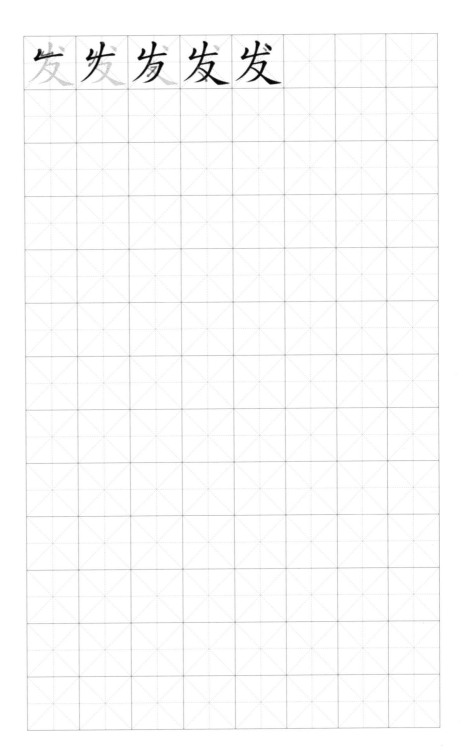

Practise writing the phrase for 'achievement' below. Well done!
You've achieved a lot by learning all these characters.

大器 achievement/
generosity (da⁴ qi⁴)

This phrase is made from
the characters for 'big'
and 'utensil'. It can also
mean 'great talent'.
For stroke order see
pp. 16 and 91.

And finally, our last character is 'end'.

末 end (mo[4])

It looks as if the topmost branches of this tree have plateaued, indicating that it has ended its growth. Make sure that the upper line is longer than the lower one!

Cover: The character for 'tree'
p2: The characters for 'wind', 'son' and 'fish'
p3: The characters for 'boat', 'stone' and 'river'
p4: The character for 'hand'

First published in the United Kingdom in 2016 by
Thames & Hudson Ltd, 181A High Holborn, London WC1V 7QX

Elements from this book were first published in *Chineasy* (2014)
and *Chineasy Everyday* (2016).

Chineasy Workbook © 2016 Chineasy Ltd (chineasy.com)

'Chineasy' is a registered word and logo trademark of ShaoLan
Hsueh, used under licence by Thames & Hudson Ltd.

Art Director: ShaoLan Hsueh 薛曉嵐
Author and Concept: ShaoLan Hsueh 薛曉嵐
Illustrator: Noma Bar

British Library Cataloguing-in-Publication Data
A catalogue record for this book is available from
the British Library

ISBN 978-0-500-42060-7

Printed in China by Reliance Printing (Shenzhen) Co. Ltd

To find out about all our publications, please visit
www.thamesandhudson.com. There you can subscribe
to our e-newsletter, browse or download our current
catalogue, and buy any titles that are in print.